J   5471933
970.3   13.95
Woo
Wood
The Crow Indians

DATE DUE			

THE
CROW
INDIANS

THE JUNIOR LIBRARY OF
AMERICAN INDIANS

THE
CROW
INDIANS

Leigh Hope Wood

CHELSEA HOUSE PUBLISHERS
New York Philadelphia

FRONTISPIECE Oo-je-en-a-he-ha (Woman Who Lives in a Bear's Den), as painted by George Catlin in 1832.

CHAPTER TITLE ORNAMENT A Crow Warrior; taken from an illustration on a 19th-century Crow robe.

Chelsea House Publishers
EDITOR-IN-CHIEF Richard S. Papale
EXECUTIVE MANAGING EDITOR Karyn Gullen Browne
COPY CHIEF Philip Koslow
PICTURE EDITOR Adrian G. Allen
ART DIRECTOR Nora Wertz
MANUFACTURING DIRECTOR Gerald Levine
SYSTEMS MANAGER Lindsey Ottman
PRODUCTION COORDINATOR Marie Claire Cebrián-Ume

The Junior Library of American Indians
SENIOR EDITOR Liz Sonneborn

Staff for THE CROW INDIANS
DEPUTY COPY CHIEF Margaret Dornfeld
EDITORIAL ASSISTANT Nicole Greenblatt
SENIOR DESIGNER Rae Grant
PICTURE RESEARCHERS Anne Bohlen, Alan Gottlieb
COVER ILLUSTRATOR Vilma Ortiz

3 5 7 9 8 6 4 2

Library of Congress Cataloging-in-Publication Data
Wood, Leigh Hope.
The Crow Indians/by Leigh Hope Wood.
  p. cm.—(The Junior Library of American Indians)
Includes index.
Summary: Discusses the life, culture, and future of the Crow Indians.
    ISBN 0-7910-1661-7
    ISBN 0-7910-1964-0 (pbk.)
1. Crow Indians—Juvenile literature. [1. Crow Indians. 2. Indians of
North America.] I. Title. II. Series.   92-18148
E99.C92W59 1993   CIP
973'.04975—dc20   AC

CONTENTS

A portrait of a Crow man, painted in 1832 by American artist George Catlin.

CHAPTER **1**

Coyote and the Ducks

Old Man Coyote felt very lonely as he gazed across the gray sea. In every direction he saw nothing but water and sky.

Then he spotted two red-eyed ducks paddling toward him. When the ducks came near, Coyote asked them if they had seen anything during their journey across the water. The ducks told him they had not. Yet they suspected something interesting might lie below the water's surface.

Excited by the thought, Coyote asked the ducks to dive down and and have a look. One duck agreed, while the other decided to stay

7

with Coyote. Coyote asked the diver to bring up anything that he could find.

The diver disappeared below the surface of the water. He soon returned, carrying something in his mouth. The other two rushed to him to see what he had.

Coyote looked at the object and told the ducks it was either a piece of root or a branch from a tree. It convinced Coyote that there were even greater things to be found at the bottom of the sea.

At Coyote's request, the diving duck again disappeared into the water. He was gone for a long time. When he reappeared, he had a lump of mud in his beak.

Coyote told his two friends that he could make something from the mud. He blew on the lump, and it grew in every direction. Within minutes, Coyote had created a large island.

The ducks begged Coyote to make the island even bigger. He blew on it a second time. The island then grew as large as the earth is today.

Coyote and the ducks paused for a moment to admire the brown prairie that stretched out to the horizon. They agreed that it was beautiful but very empty.

One duck suggested that the prairie would be nicer if something lived there. Coyote nodded and picked up the root that the diver had brought him. From it, Coyote made grass, trees, and all the other plants of the earth.

Seeing what Coyote could do, the other duck squealed with excitement and offered his own suggestion. He thought the prairie needed canyons and valleys. The duck asked Coyote to make some rivers. The water would cut into the earth, and then the land would not be so flat.

Coyote liked this idea. Here and there, he pushed the earth aside, creating riverbeds where water could flow. The ducks were very pleased. They declared that the land was perfect.

Yet Coyote still felt lonely. He thought that the three of them should have companions. From a handful of earth, Coyote made men.

The ducks were amazed by these new creatures, but they wanted to have their own companions. As a favor to his two brothers, Coyote made ducks of all kinds.

He was very pleased with his creations until he realized that he had forgotten to make women. Men would be content and prosper only if female humans lived with them on the earth. Coyote took more of the mud and shaped it into women. He also made female ducks.

Old Man Coyote continued his work. When he was finished, the earth had shape and was filled with all sorts of living things.

For hundreds of years, the Crow Indians have told this story to their children. From the tale, youngsters learn how the Crows came

A view of the Crow homeland.

to live in their land on the grassy prairies of what is now the state of Montana. The Crows feel very lucky that Coyote and the two ducks gave them such a beautiful home.

Throughout their history, the Crows have welcomed visitors into their homeland. Some outsiders have been grateful for their hospitality. But others—seeing a lush land covered with clear rivers and mountain forests and teeming with wildlife—wanted to take over Crow territory.

The Crows have always fiercely fought off attempts to steal their land. Unfortunately, they could not win every battle. Over the years, they lost portions of their territory. But the heart of Crow country still belongs to the Crow people.

More than 8,000 Crows now live there. Others reside in cities across the United States but return to Montana whenever they can. Seeing the homeland again, they remember Old Man Coyote's special gift to them and feel blessed to call themselves Crows. ▲

A Crow girl and her mother, photographed in 1908.

CHAPTER 2

Coming Together

The ancestors of the Crows lived on the Great Plains for thousands of years. This area of flat, dry land lies in the center of what is now the United States.

The first Indians of the Plains survived by hunting animals and gathering wild plants. They had to travel constantly, following herds and searching for ripe fruits and vegetables. Wherever they could find food, they made their home.

About 1,800 years ago, these people began to farm corn. In order to tend their crops, they had to stay in one place for long stretches of time.

At first, their corn harvests were only a small part of their food supply. But as the Indians became better farmers, their crops grew larger. Eventually they grew enough corn to store part of the crop for winter. Their survival no longer depended on finding game and wild plants.

In time, the Indians began searching for more fertile farmland. Some migrated north. By the year 1000, Indians had established farming settlements along the Missouri River in what is now North Dakota. The people in these settlements lived in villages of large dome-shaped lodges made of wood, grass, and earth.

Although they obtained most of their food from farming, some villagers often traveled through the Great Plains to hunt the great herds of buffalo there. In the 1500s, small groups of hunters from the Missouri River settlements began to spend the entire winter on the Plains. The longer they stayed there, the more independent they became from their relatives.

Some of these hunters eventually decided to stay on the Plains for good. They settled in the valley of the Yellowstone River. The Crow Indians trace their ancestry to one of these groups, called the Awatixa Hidatsa. These

The Crows' ancestors lived in villages of dome-shaped lodges made of earth.

people later became known as the Mountain Crows.

In the early 1700s, the Mountain Crows acquired horses from other Indians to the south. At that time, horses were new to many parts of North America. Spanish explorers had brought the animals to the continent from Europe only about 150 years earlier.

The Mountain Crows prized their horses. On horseback, hunters could chase down their prey more easily. The animals also allowed the Indians to travel farther and faster than before.

Soon after the Mountain Crows obtained horses, another group of Hidatsa people from the Missouri Valley moved to the Plains. They became the River Crows. Although they lived north of the Yellowstone River along the upper reaches of the Missouri, they visited the Mountain Crows often.

The two groups shared many things. They spoke the same language and held the same religious beliefs. Both peoples told similar stories about Old Man Coyote.

Eventually Mountain Crows and River Crows began to marry one another and have children. By 1750, the two groups had become so interrelated that they no longer thought of themselves as separate peoples. They had become one *tribe*—the *Absaroka*. (The name, which meant "Children of the Long-beaked Bird," was later translated by non-Indians as "Crows.")

The Crows did not have a written language. Therefore, there are no records of what they thought or how they lived when they first became a united people. In the early 1800s, however, white people began to visit the Crows and write about their experiences among the Indians. From these writings, it is possible to piece together a picture of Crow life long ago.

LOCATIONS OF THE CROWS AND THEIR NEIGHBORS IN ABOUT 1750

(modern state and international boundaries)

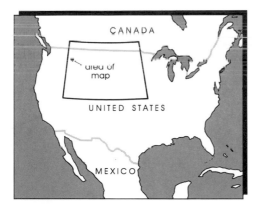

Unlike their Hidatsa kin, the Crows were not a settled, farming people. Instead, they preferred to travel from place to place, their movements guided by the seasons. Because they were constantly on the move, it was impossible for all the many Crows to live together. They broke into small groups, called *bands*, each of which had its own temporary camp.

Each camp was made up of groups of *tipis*. These dwellings were constructed from a wooden frame covered with animal skins. The tipis were well suited to the life of a mobile people because they could be set up and taken down very quickly.

In the winter, Crow bands camped along the upper Missouri River or in the valleys of the Rocky Mountains. The geography of these regions protected them from cold winds and snow.

In the spring, the bands traveled to areas where turnips, rhubarb, and strawberries grew wild. A few months later, they searched out chokecherry bushes and plum trees covered with ripe fruit.

All year long, individuals and small parties hunted rabbit, deer, elk, and other game. But in the summer, bands united for great buffalo hunts. Such occasions allowed the Crows to visit with friends and family.

Every Crow had many relatives. Each person in the tribe belonged to a *clan*, which was made up of several families. Clan members felt very closely tied to one another. In fact, they were considered so intimately related that a man and woman of the same clan could not marry. People of different clans

Two Crow women picking wild choke-cherries, a favorite food of the tribe.

always traveled together so that no one would have to look outside his or her own camp to find a mate.

The decision as to when and to where Crow bands should move was made by warrior societies. In the 1800s, the most prominent societies were the Foxes and the

Riding on swift horses, Crow men became great buffalo hunters.

Lumpwood. Some others were called the Big Dogs, the Muddy Hands, and the Ravens.

Their members were young men who distinguished themselves in battle. The Crows valued skilled warriors because they often needed to defend their homeland. The lands they controlled included such rich hunting grounds that other Indian tribes frequently invaded Crow territory.

The members of warrior societies competed with each other for honor and glory. In public parades, warrior society members boasted of their successes. They also teased warriors from societies that had fallen short.

Each society established its own customs and chose its own leaders. To be a warrior society leader, a man had to do four things. He had to lead a war party, capture an enemy's horse, be the first to touch an enemy in battle, and snatch an enemy's weapon. A warrior who achieved these feats was called a *bachecitche*, which meant "good man." Non-Indians usually called these men chiefs.

The Crows had other leaders with different responsibilities. The elders of a clan or of a household were often called upon to settle family disputes or advise the chiefs. Holy men and women were in charge of performing religious ceremonies, although it was up to the chiefs to schedule these events.

The most common ceremony performed by the Crows was the vision quest. In this ritual, a young man left his home and traveled alone to a remote area. There he prayed, asking the Creator for guidance. On a successful vision quest, a spirit would appear and offer the boy instructions on how to live his life. Spirits usually took the form of an animal, such as a bear or a buffalo.

The Sun Dance was another important ceremony. The ritual was held in the summer and centered around a warrior who wanted revenge for the death of a friend or close relative in battle. With the other participants, the warrior danced to the beating of drums and the singing of onlookers. During his dance, the warrior fell into a trance, in which he saw a vision that gave him the confidence to punish his enemy. Other dancers could also be inspired by a vision and agree to join the warrior on his mission.

Every year, a special ceremony was held, during which the Crows planted tobacco seeds. (The Crows believed tobacco was a sacred gift from the Creator.) The responsibility for supervising this ritual fell to the members of the Tobacco Society. These men and women came from all of the Crow bands.

The Tobacco Society and other religious groups also instructed Crow children. From them, youngsters learned about Crow beliefs and the meaning of rituals. Adults told boys and girls to imitate their elders, who could teach them how to behave properly.

Boys learned how to track animals and scout for enemies. These skills prepared

them for adulthood. As men, they would have to defend their camp, raid their enemies, and lead their band to new hunting grounds.

Girls were taught how to butcher buffalo and tan hides. They also learned how to make clothing, tools, and tipi covers. As women, they would be in charge of their family's home.

Cleaning and stretching buffalo hides was one of the many jobs of Crow women.

At an early age, Crow children discovered which tasks they were expected to perform. But they were also taught to respect people whose talents were different from those expected. For instance, if a woman rode a horse skillfully, she earned the right to ride with the warriors. Likewise, a man could stay home and perform household work if he wanted. In fact, a group of men called *bate* preferred to dress and live as women. The Crows believed these men enjoyed a special tie to the Creator.

The Crow people lived in an ordered society. They remained true to their customs, followed their leaders, and felt close ties to their family and clan. But in the early 19th century, a new race of people came to the Great Plains and challenged the order of the Crows' way of life. ▲

A gathering of Plains Indians, painted in 1833. In the distance stands Fort Union.

CHAPTER **3**

Strangers Arrive

In the early 1800s, non-Indians began to arrive in Crow territory. These people came for several different reasons. Among the first newcomers were *fur traders*. They were looking for the chance to trade with the Indians and, often, for adventure. Following them were settlers, traveling in covered wagons. Settlers came west in search of a new home and a new life.

No matter what their motives, the newcomers all had similar effects on the Crows. They introduced the Indians to new customs and ideas. And this experience changed the

Indians' own way of life, usually for the worse.

The Crows had heard of non-Indians well before they first met them. Other Indians had been dealing with whites for hundreds of years. Especially in what is now the north-eastern United States, Indians and non-Indians had long been trading partners.

European and American traders were eager to obtain animal furs from Indian hunters. Non-Indians would pay high prices for fur hats and coats, so these fur traders could make large profits. In exchange, the Indians received machine made goods, such as metal tools and guns, from the traders.

At first, the fur trade seemed to be good business for everyone involved. But, unfortunately, non-Indians brought more than foreign goods to Indian populations. Many traders were carriers of European diseases, such as smallpox and measles.

The carriers often did not appear ill. Whites had been exposed to the diseases for a long time. Their bodies had developed a natural resistance to the viruses. As a result, infected whites did not always become sick.

Indians, on the other hand, had no way of fighting off European diseases. When a group of Indians first came in contact with a carrier, many fell ill and died. And infected Indians unknowingly gave the viruses to family, friends, and other tribes. In some cases, entire tribes were wiped out within just a few years.

In the late 1700s, outbreaks of smallpox began to strike the Indians of the Great Plains. The disease spread quickly among the Crows. This was especially true during the winter, when small groups of tribespeople shared close quarters.

The Crows, however, soon learned how to contain an outbreak. Whenever someone became infected, the Crows split into smaller groups that then scattered in different directions. In this way, some groups were able to isolate themselves from a virus.

François Antoine Larocque, one of the Crows' first non-Indian visitors, wrote that the tribe had been hard hit by disease. Nevertheless, in 1805, when Larocque entered their territory, they were still a very powerful people.

Larocque came west to trade with the Crows. To establish a friendship with their chiefs, he offered them an impressive array of gifts: knives, axes, steel awls (tools for making holes in leather), decorative glass beads, musket balls, and musket powder.

The design on this parfleche (leather satchel) was carved by a Crow woman using a steel awl.

This quiver (a container for arrows) is decorated with glass beads that the Crows obtained from non-Indian traders.

(From Indian traders of other tribes, the Crows had probably already obtained muskets.)

The Crows welcomed these goods. They saw that, in many ways, they were better than the tools and other objects they made themselves. For instance, metal tools stayed sharper and broke less often than implements that Crows fashioned from stone or bone.

The new goods also helped them perform their work in less time. Crow women particularly liked steel awls. To make clothing and tipi covers, they had to sew together pieces of hide. Steel awls could poke holes in the tough leather far easier than the needle-like tools they used to make by hand.

Non-Indian goods also gave the Crows new ways of decorating the objects they created from leather. Using steel awls, women carved intricate designs on leather traveling packs called parfleches. With brightly colored glass beads, they adorned their clothing.

Probably the trade items most valued by the Crows were muskets, balls, and powder. Muskets proved the ideal weapon for battle because they could kill an enemy at a great distance. However, these guns did not entirely replace the Crow's bows and arrows.

Hunters still found a bow easier to handle when riding alongside a herd of stampeding buffalo. Warriors on raids also preferred their old weapons because the sound of a gun might alert an entire enemy camp of an attack.

The year following Larocque's visit, a party of American explorers came to Crow territory. They had been sent by President Thomas Jefferson to look for a water route from the Mississippi River to the Pacific Ocean. They were also to gather information about the land that lay between the Mississippi and the Rocky Mountains. Known to non-Indians as the Louisiana Purchase, this area had recently been bought by the United States from France. It included the Crow homeland.

Jefferson appointed Meriwether Lewis and William Clark to head the expedition of 43 frontiersmen. During their travels, none of them encountered the Crows. However, after the exploration was over, one man named John Colter decided to return to Crow country to trade with the tribe. He spent the winter of 1806–7 along the banks of the Yellowstone River.

The next summer Colter joined up with several other traders. Near the mouth of the Bighorn River, they built a two-room log

continued on page 41

SHIELDS AND SPIRITS

Crow warriors took great care in making the shields they carried into battle. Made from animal skins, the shields were often painted with colorful pictures and patterns.

Many of these paintings were very beautiful. But to the Crows, they were much more than mere decoration. Usually, the images represented something the painter had seen in a vision.

Visions often appeared to young Crow men during a ritual called a vision quest. After traveling to a remote area, a man on a vision quest would pray for a long time. If the ritual was a success, a spirit, usually in the form of an animal, would appear before him. The spirit would tell the man how to live his life and pass on to him power and strength.

The Crows knew that their shields alone could not fend off arrows and bullets. But the images painted on them made warriors feel well protected. In the paintings, the Crows believed they captured some of the special power of their spirit guides.

A Crow shield painted with an image of one bear attacking another that has a human hand emerging from its mouth.

A storm cloud emitting lightning bolts is painted on this shield, which belonged to a warrior named Bull Snake. The black lines at the bottom represent bullets shooting skyward. The eagle feathers, crane's head, and piece of rawhide in the shape of a buffalo gave special strength to the shield's owner.

bottom of the shield, a buffalo bull is shown pursuing a buffalo
cow into the cloud.

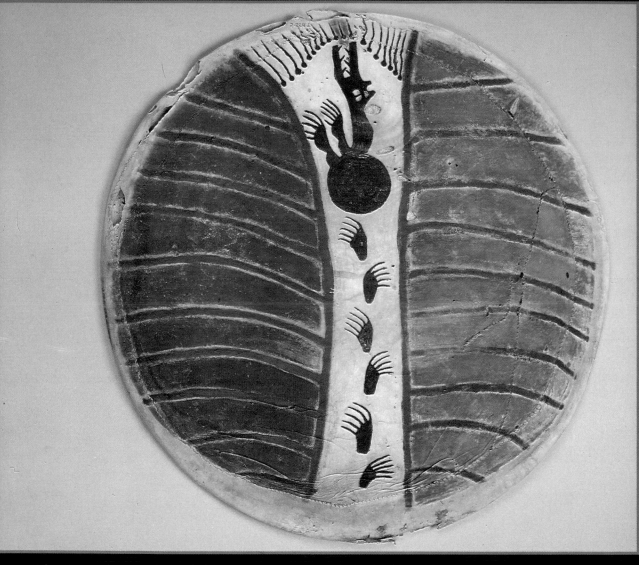

The Crow often made buckskin covers to protect their shields. This cover is painted with a scene of an angry bear being shot by 19 bullets as it rushes from its den toward its attacker. According to the shield's owner, Big Bear, the green half of the cover represents the earth, and the red half, the sky.

Last owned by a man called Shavings, this shield depicts a group of
stars in the dawn sky. The stars are represented by a clawlike figure
above a black line (the darkness of night) and a red area (dawn).
The two eagle feathers were meant to make Shavings swift.

71725-2

*Bull That Goes Hunting made this shield to represent his vision of
a giant buffalo bull standing astride the Pryor Mountains as it de-
fies its enemies. Three bullet holes testify that the shield was used
in battle.*

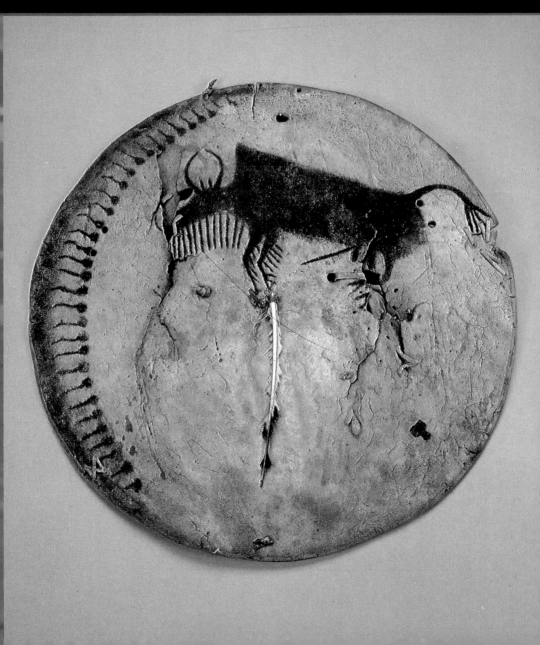

This shield originally belonged to Eelapuash (Sore Belly), one of the greatest Crow warriors. Attached to it are two squirrel skins to make Eelapuash quick, a weasel skin to make him watchful, and several eagle feathers to give him power.

A man named Kiss owned this shield. Its four red circles represent sun dogs—the circles that appear around the sun before a storm. The black lines are pieces of a man that are so small his enemies cannot touch him.

Bull Tongue carried this shield into many battles against the Sioux. The four red crane tracks ensured that this bird would protect him.

continued from page 32

cabin, which they named Fort Raymond. At this post, the men traded with the Crows year-round. In 1807 and 1808 they pushed farther into Crow territory. They discovered rich trapping grounds and the places where the tribe gathered to visit and trade.

One of the traders, Edward Rose, tried to become friends with the Crows before attempting to barter with them. A man of white, black, and Cherokee Indian descent, Rose had observed that the Crows greatly valued generosity. To encourage their friendship, he gave presents to all their important chiefs.

When Rose's boss found out what he had done, he scolded his employee. Rose then quit and went to live permanently among his Crow friends. To him, the Crows were far more "civilized" than non-Indians.

Fort Raymond was abandoned in 1811, but soon other men came to Crow territory to trade. Between 1821 and 1852, fur traders built several posts at the mouth of the Bighorn River. Like Rose, several chose to live with the Indians.

Among these men was James Beckwourth, a black fur trader. After he had returned to the East, Beckwourth claimed that he had married a Crow woman and even led the Crows into battle. It was through his and other traders' stories that eastern

George Catlin's sketch
of Crow chief Red Bear.

Americans first learned about the Crow people.

Competition in the fur trade greatly affected the Crows. Other Indian tribes, who had killed all the fur-bearing animals in their lands, began flocking to Crow territory, where beaver and buffalo were still plentiful. The more trappers that came to the region, the fewer animals there were in the Crow hunting grounds.

In the 1840s, tribes from the eastern Great Plains had another reason for invading the homeland of the Crows. At this time, wagon trains of non-Indian travelers began to flock westward. Some were headed for California, where gold had been discovered. Others were bound for the rich farmland of western Oregon. But still others chose to settle on the eastern Plains. They established home-steads there with little thought that they were taking over lands that had been ruled by Indians for centuries.

The Indians who lived there, the Sioux and Cheyennes, had to make a difficult decision. If they fought the invaders, they would de-stroy the trade alliances they had made with non-Indians. But so many settlers were com-ing that they could not remain in their home-lands without a confrontation.

They chose to move to other Indians' territory. Many of the Sioux began to trespass on Crow hunting grounds. At the same time, Blackfoot Indians in Oregon Territory moved onto the western edge of Crow land. Like the Sioux, they were being driven from their home by white settlers.

As the Crows began to make war on these invaders, officials in the U.S. government became anxious. They feared the fighting among tribes would threaten the safe passage of non-Indians to the Pacific Coast. They were also afraid that American settlers would become too scared to build homesteads on the Great Plains. The government wanted Americans to live there. The settlers' presence would strengthen the United States's claim to the region.

In 1851, the government decided to intervene. It invited thousands of Crow, Sioux, Blackfoot, Shoshone, and Cheyenne Indians to a peace council at Fort Laramie in present-day Wyoming. The officials who organized that council wanted to determine borders for each tribe's territory. They hoped that if everyone agreed upon exactly which areas belonged to which peoples, the fighting would stop.

At the Fort Laramie council, official borders for the Crow territory were set for the first time. The area was bounded on the east by the Powder River, on the west by the Yellowstone, on the north by the Missouri and Musselshell, and on the south by the Wind River Mountains.

The United States's definition of Crow territory was about the same as the tribe's. Although the Crows kept their land, they lost something perhaps even more valuable—control over their own world. At Fort Laramie, a foreign government told the Crows where they could and could not live.

The meeting marked a new era for the Crow leadership. Crow leaders were no longer simply those who had the respect of their people. Leaders now had to be able to deal with non-Indian traders and government officials. At the same time, they had do everything possible to protect their lands from outsiders—non-Indians and Indians alike. In the years to come, that challenge would prove nearly impossible to meet. ▲

Crow Indians watching
as the last spike is driven
into the rails of the Northern Pacific Railroad in
1883.

CHAPTER **4**

Trying Times

The late 1800s in the Great Plains saw the arrival of more non-Indians than ever before. Many came for jobs working on the railroads, which, once built, would connect the eastern and western United States. Others came to mine for gold. Still others came to farm.

Whatever the newcomers did, it interfered with Plains Indians' lives. Miners trespassed on their territory. Farmers plowed and built fences on their hunting grounds. But the railroad workers caused the worst problems. The railroad lines ran through the areas where buffalo herds roamed. As a result, the herds were being scattered, making it more difficult for the Indians to hunt for a living.

As Plains Indians' lands became more crowded, their anger toward the U.S. government grew. The Indians had agreed to the government's boundaries for their territories established by the 1851 Fort Laramie treaty. Now the United States was ignoring the very borders it had set. The government knew non-Indians were crossing these boundaries onto Indian land but refused to do anything about it.

The Teton Sioux were perhaps hurt most by the government's neglect. Their hunting grounds lay in the direct path of the westward-moving settlers.

By the summer of 1866, the Teton Sioux had had enough. They declared war on the U.S. forts that lined the Bozeman Trail. This road connected Fort Laramie and the goldfields of present-day Montana. After the violence erupted, the trail earned the nickname "the Bloody Bozeman."

Red Cloud, a great Teton Sioux chief, asked the Crows' warriors to join in the fight. The Crows flatly refused. They knew that many of their Indian enemies had already been pushed off their land by non-Indians. The Crows hoped that if they remained on good terms with the U.S. government, they might avoid having the same thing happen to them. The tribe was also unwilling to ally themselves with their Indian enemies to battle whites. In the Crows' eyes, the Sioux were far more dangerous than non-Indians.

One U.S. soldier, Lieutenant William Templeton, wrote about his experiences with the Crows during the war. He was stationed at Fort C. F. Smith, the westernmost fort on the Bozeman Trail.

One day in August 1866, the troops at the post spied a group of warriors on the opposite side of the Bighorn River. When the Indians began shouting at the soldiers, a few troops, including Templeton, rode out to meet them. The Indians were well armed, and the soldiers were nervous.

Several of the warriors began to speak, but not knowing any Indian languages, Templeton had no idea what they were saying. Finally, he heard one word he understood: *Absaroka.* Suddenly, he and his fellow soldiers felt at ease. They realized that the Indians were Crows and therefore were friends of the soldiers.

The next day, the leaders of the warriors and several soldiers met. First, the chiefs welcomed the white men to their homeland. Then, they told them the whereabouts of a nearby Sioux camp. With this gesture, the Crows made it clear they were on the U.S. Army's side in the war. The meeting ended with the Crows and the whites agreeing to live with each other in peace.

The war continued until 1868, when the United States admitted defeat. U.S. officials, Teton Sioux chiefs, and representatives of some other Plains tribes gathered at Fort Laramie to negotiate a treaty of peace.

As the winners in the war, the Teton Sioux were in a good position to make demands. The government promised to abandon all its forts along the "Bloody Bozeman." It also assured the Sioux that they could hunt in the Powder River valley. This area was just to the east of Crow territory.

The deal frightened the Crow chiefs. The beaten United States was giving the tribe's enemies everything they wanted. It looked as though the Crows' friendship with the U.S. Army did not count for much with the treaty officials.

The spokesman for the Crow chiefs was named Sits in the Middle of the Land. He was afraid that the officials might try to seize all of the tribe's land. With this in mind, he agreed to give a huge tract of Crow land—nearly 30 million acres—to the United States. In return, the officials promised the Crows that they could keep 8 million acres in the Bighorn Valley forever. This land became the Crow Indian Reservation. (A *reservation* is a tract

An 1837 painting of Indian traders in the courtyard at Fort Laramie.

set aside by the government for the use of Indians only.)

The treaty spelled out the new boundaries for Crow territory. To the north and west, the tribe's homeland stretched to the Yellowstone River. This natural boundary was understood and respected by the Crows. The southern and eastern borders were just lines that the U.S. officials drew on a map. To the Crows, maps held no meaning. Unknowingly, they constantly crossed these boundaries as they followed their old hunting paths.

The fighting between Plains Indians and the U.S. Army did not end with the war on the Bozeman Trail. More and more settlers came to the region, prompting more and more attacks by the Indians there.

The Crows tried to stay out of the Plains wars. A few Crow warriors joined the U.S.

Army as scouts, but most of the tribespeople remained neutral. Their greatest concern was holding on to the small part of their homeland that the 1868 treaty called Crow territory.

The U.S. government had made several other promises to the Crows in the treaty. It was to provide the tribe with a carpenter, an engineer, a farmer, a blacksmith, a doctor, and a teacher. The government would also build a school on Crow land and donate food and tools to the tribe. An official known as an *agent* would hand out these goods and supervise the workers.

Agents had still another responsibility. They were to teach Indians about how white people lived. The government hoped that Indians would then willingly give up their own way of life. If they did, officials thought, Indians would stop fighting the whites who were taking over Indian land.

The Crows' agents tried to persuade them to make their living by farming, as most white settlers did. But most had little interest in becoming farmers. Growing crops was hard and boring work. The Crows much preferred the excitement of the hunt.

A few Crow chiefs, however, took the agents' pleas more seriously and tried to farm. Among them were Iron Bull, Medicine

Crow, and Plenty Coups. Like the rest of the Crows, these leaders loved their old way of life. But they also knew their world was changing quickly. They believed that it was time to learn some new ways as well.

In 1880, the government invited six Crow chiefs, including these three leaders, to Washington, D.C. The Crows met with the official in charge of the Bureau of Indian Affairs (BIA). (This part of the government handled all dealings between Indians and the United States.) The chiefs also spoke with President Rutherford B. Hayes.

The chiefs were surprised by the officials' request: they wanted the Crows to give up still more land. Feeling they had no choice, the chiefs sold 1.5 million acres. They also agreed to allow the Northern Pacific Railroad to lay tracks in their territory. The railroad would bring even more whites westward.

Among the newcomers were *missionaries*. These people wanted Indians to take up still another white custom—the Christian religion. The first missionaries in Crow territory, were two Catholic priests named Father Pierpaolo Prando and Father Peter Barcelo. In 1887, they built St. Xavier Mission on the banks of the Bighorn River.

After learning the Crow language, Prando translated hymns and portions of the Bible.

BOUNDARIES OF CROW TERRITORY IN 1851 AND 1868

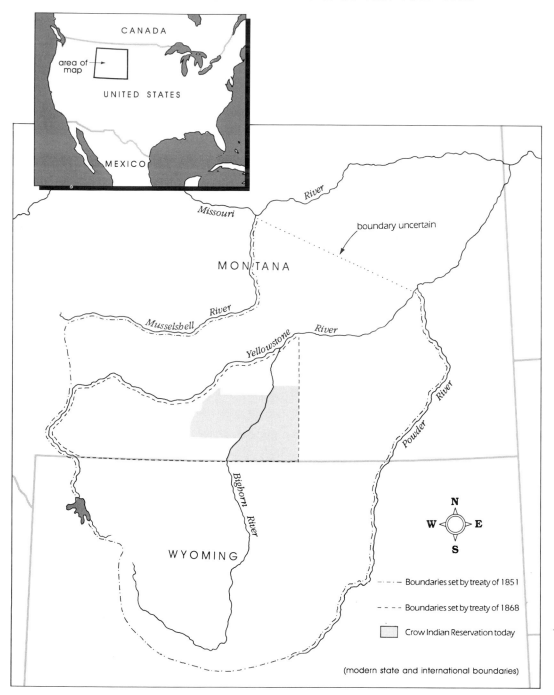

CANADA

area of map

UNITED STATES

MEXICO

River

Missouri

boundary uncertain

MONTANA

Musselshell River

Yellowstone River

Bighorn River

Powder River

WYOMING

N
W E
S

- · - · — Boundaries set by treaty of 1851

- - - — Boundaries set by treaty of 1868

Crow Indian Reservation today

(modern state and international boundaries)

Many of the Crows listened to him as he preached. Unlike most agents, Prando earned their respect. He was honest and seemed to care about the Crow people.

Many tribespeople chose to attend the church at St. Xavier. Few, however, supported the school set up at Crow Agency, the area where the agent lived. Beginning in 1884, all Crow children over the age of six were required to go there. In time, older children were taken from their families and forced to go to boarding schools. Some of these schools were as far away as Pennsylvania.

Life was difficult for the boarding school students. They had to wear uniforms and learn their lessons in English, which was to most a completely foreign language. When they were not in class, they were expected to work long hours in the school kitchen or laundry. The hard labor and unclean facilities made many of the children ill.

But, perhaps worst of all, these students were separated from their families for long periods of time. They could not watch their elders and learn from them. Far away from the Crow world, they could no longer take comfort and pride in being part of their mighty people. ▲

Agents giving rations of meat to women on the Crow Indian Reservation in 1893.

CHAPTER 5

A Safe Prison

As time passed, the Crows adapted to reservation life. As more Crows became settled farmers, the freedom of riding the open plains came to exist only in the memories of older tribe members.

In some respects, the Crows finally had a safe home. At last, they were far removed from the anguish and violence of the Plains wars. But the agents' rules also prohibited many of the ceremonies and customs that Crows held dear. In this way, the reservation was little better than a prison.

The young men of the tribe were perhaps the most frustrated. Without an agent's permission, they were not permitted to leave the reservation. They were no longer free to raid their enemies' camps and thus prove their manhood with their war exploits. And unable to go on vision quests, they could not meet their special spirit guide who could tell them how to live as men.

In the summer of 1887, a group of Northern Cheyennes invited some young Crows to their annual Sun Dance. The Cheyennes were holding the ceremony in defiance of government agents. The boys were thrilled by the invitation. At last they would have a way of displaying their bravery to their people.

During the Sun Dance, young men asked for blessings from the Creator. As a sacrifice, they sliced pieces of flesh from their bodies. They also made cuts in the skin of their chests and threaded rawhide strings through these holes. After tying the string to a pole, they leaned back until the string was tight. Eventually the string broke through their skin. The ritual was very painful. By enduring it, the men proved themselves to be courageous.

One young Crow was particularly brave at the Northern Cheyennes' Sun Dance. He was known as Wraps Up His Tail. To show their admiration, his hosts offered him a saber and a new name—Sword Bearer.

The honor gave Sword Bearer new confidence. He told everyone of his pride in his people's traditions. Despite the agents' demands, Sword Bearer refused to walk behind a plow or go to a government school.

Some of the older Crows encouraged Sword Bearer. They had grown tired of the way the agents treated them. Obedience no longer seemed the right path to follow. They told Sword Bearer to act as he judged best.

Later that summer, Sword Bearer led 22 men in a raid on some Blackfoot Indians who had stolen Crow horses. When the group returned, they celebrated their victory as their fathers had. Riding through their camp, they yelled and fired their rifles into the air.

Sword Bearer felt freer than he ever had before. Carried away with emotion, he shot a round of bullets into the agent's house and a nearby store.

As Sword Bearer and his men rode off, the terrified agent telegraphed his superiors in Washington. He asked them to send troops to protect Crow Agency. The agent's fear spread to local settlers. Their newspapers warned all non-Indians to prepare for another Indian war.

U.S. Army troops soon arrived on the reservation. Many Crows then moved their tipis closer to the agency. They wanted to show that they only wished to keep the peace.

Sword Bearer, however, would not submit. When soldiers tried to arrest him, the young warrior put up a fight. The soldiers opened fire. Sword Bearer and eight other Crows were killed.

The conflict was the Crows' final battle. Afterward, agents became even stricter in their enforcement of the government's rules. Before, the Crows had to obtain their agent's permission to leave the reservation. Now they were not even allowed to move freely inside the reservation borders. All Crows were told to choose one place to settle.

Many Crows continued to live at Crow Agency. But others founded new communities, including Pryor, Black Lodge, Lodge Grass, and Wyola.

While the Crows were forming these settlements, the U.S. government began to ask the tribe to give up still more land. In agreements made in 1892 and 1904, the Crow chiefs were forced to sign over nearly 3 million acres. The United States bought this land at a bargain price—an average of only about 65 cents per acre.

At the same time, the government had another plan for gaining control of Crow country as well as other Indian lands. In 1887, the U.S. Congress passed the General Allotment Act. This law allowed the government

The Crow community of St. Xavier, photographed in 1890.

to divide Indian lands into small plots called *allotments*. Allotments would be owned by individuals. Previously, most Indian people shared all of their land.

Some well-meaning white Americans pressured officials into adopting the allotment policy. They thought that Indians could hold on to their land more easily if they had deeds to small tracts, as white settlers did.

However, the government saw allotment in a different light. According to the General Allotment Act, each Indian on a reservation was entitled to a specific number of acres. After all Indians were given their allotments, any leftover land became the property of the United States. In this way, the government could take over Indian land without even paying for it.

Understandably, the Crows did not want allotments. They wanted to continue to share their land as they always had. For years, they fought the policy. But, by 1904, the tribe realized that this was one fight they could not win. Most Crow people then agreed to choose an allotment.

Slowly, Crow families began to build cabins and farms on their allotments. Often, these homesteads were far away from those of their family and friends. Wanting to stay close, many Crows made a special effort to visit loved ones frequently.

The tribe also held on fiercely to old ways that helped keep them united. In the summer, groups of Crows left their homes and headed for the Bighorn Mountains. Escaping the heat of the prairies, they gathered berries and renewed ties with one another. In the fall and spring, the Tobacco Society continued to

A women's horse race held at one of the first Crow fairs.

hold dances and to initiate new members. In the winter, communities formed teams and played the hand game, a traditional Crow contest. To cheer on the players, crowds of men and women sang and drummed. And on holidays, such as Christmas and Independence Day, the Crows took the opportunity to camp and feast together.

In 1904, the Crows' agents began to organize a new annual gathering—the agricultural fair. At the fair, the Crows were to display their farm products. The most impressive were to win prizes. The tribe had little interest in a farm show. Gradually, they introduced to the fair new events that they enjoyed. Among these were parades, horse racing, dancing, and Tobacco Society meetings.

The agents tolerated most of these changes. However, they continued to discourage the Tobacco Society meetings and all other rituals of the Crows' religion. Missionaries supported the agents' efforts.

Some Crows still belonged to Christian churches. But most wanted to keep their old ceremonies alive. In fact, some rituals that had almost been forgotten were revived at this time. These rituals not only linked the Crows to their ancestors. They also held them together as a people. ◣

Plenty Coups was the last great traditional chief of the Crow people.

CHAPTER **6**

Looking to the Future

In the late 1800s, the Crows tried to learn to live in the ever-changing present while holding onto the past. This effort can best be seen in the life of one of their chiefs—Plenty Coups. Plenty Coups knew how to deal with the non-Indian world, but never for a moment lost his pride in being a Crow.

Many times, Plenty Coups traveled to Washington to ask officials to aid the Crow people. Unlike many Indian leaders, Plenty Coups knew how the government worked. If an official was not paying enough attention to his demands, he would seek out the official's political rivals. They would be eager to hear what Plenty Coups had to say.

On the reservation, the chief showed a great respect for the old ways. He was active in the Tobacco Society and often danced at ceremonies. At his death in 1932, Plenty Coups was recognized as the last great traditional chief of his people.

The young men who took over Plenty Coups's role were very different. They could not remember the days when the Crows moved freely throughout the Great Plains. They had grown up on the reservation and had been educated in government schools. They felt as comfortable around whites as they did around their own people.

The most important of these new leaders was Robert Yellowtail. As a young man, he served as a translator to the older chiefs who could not speak English. Traveling with them to Washington, Yellowtail developed the skills needed to become a modern politician.

In 1911, the government allowed the Crows to form a business committee. Its members were to be elected by the Crow people and would represent the tribe in all official business. Yellowtail soon dominated the group.

In the 1920s, the business committee was replaced by a general council. At first, an audience of tribe members came to council meetings just to watch. But, as time went by, they became more involved in the proceedings. The audience eventually had as much say in committee decisions as the elected leaders.

In 1934, Robert Yellowtail was selected to be the superintendent (the modern term for agent) of the Crow Indian Reservation. At last, a Crow was in charge of tribal affairs. Yellowtail's position and the growing power of the council made the Crows feel more in control of their future than they had for many decades.

No longer governed by outsiders, the Crows felt freer than ever on the reservation. They practiced the religion of their choice. They traveled and visited other Crows as they wished. And they followed traditional ways without worrying about the disapproval of non-Indians.

The tribe displayed their new confidence in 1935. In that year, the government offered many Indian groups the chance to write their own constitution. U.S. officials thought all Indians would be eager to take this step. Many tribes were, but the Crows were suspicious. They knew that a constitution might make the Crows' tribal government seem

more legitimate in non-Indians' eyes. However, they did not like the idea that the docu-
ment would have to follow guidelines set by
the government. In the end, the Crows decided that their council was operating just
fine without a constitution. Proudly, they re-
jected the government's offer.

Today, the general council still governs the
reservation. Since its formation, the group
has striven to better the Crows' standard of
living. One of its goals has been increasing
the tribe's independence by improving the
Crow economy.

Past leaders (including Plenty Coups and
Robert Yellowtail) encouraged the Crows to
be farmers and ranchers. But for most people
in the tribe it was impossible to be successful
in these professions. They did not have the
money to buy the cattle, tools, and seeds
they needed. And local white-run banks
would not lend funds to Indians. Unable to do
much with their land themselves, many
Crows sold or rented their allotments to non-
Indians.

But other types of jobs have been difficult
to find on the reservation. The council has
tried to solve the problem by starting its own
businesses, but few have been successful.
The Crows find it hard to compete with non-

Indian businessmen, who often have more experience and better training.

There are some job opportunities on and off the reservation, however. A few Crows are hired by the tribal government as social workers and reservation policemen. Some also have jobs running programs to improve

Some Crows now find work as cowboys.

the tribe's health care, education, and housing. These programs are funded by the U.S. government.

Other Crows work for non-Indians. They are employed as cowboys, waitresses, and farmhands. Coal companies that mine on tribal land often hire Crows as equipment operators, clerks, and supervisors.

Jobs for teachers are found at Little Bighorn Community College. At this school, Crow students can take courses in their tribe's history and language.

Most youngsters, however, still learn about what it means to be a Crow from their elders. The Tobacco Society continues to hold meetings, dances, and ceremonies. And hand game players from various communities compete with each other in the fall and winter.

During the summer, the Crows now perform the Sun Dance. After Sword Bearer's murder, the goverment outlawed this ceremony. It was revived by a Crow religious leader, William Big Day.

In the summer of 1938, Big Day traveled to the Wind River Reservation in Wyoming. There, he witnessed a Shoshone Sun Dance. Even though it was the first he had ever seen, the songs sung by the participants seemed very familiar. Big Day then remembered that he had heard them in his dreams. He also recalled that his dreams had told him that these songs would bring happiness to the Crows.

Big Day asked the Shoshones to teach him how to perform a Sun Dance. Years passed before he felt he was ready. Finally, with the approval of Robert Yellowtail, he held a Sun Dance near Pryor in 1941. The Crows have performed this ancient ceremony several times a year ever since.

The Crow Fair, which is held the third weekend in August, is another social event that brings Crow families and friends together. Today, it is also attended by thousands of Indians and non-Indians from many states. Many outsiders are attracted by the hundreds of tipis the Crows erect near Crow Agency for the event. The Crows boast that during the fair, their reservation is the "tipi capital of the world."

The tribe also takes pride in its local high school basketball teams. At their games, the players' relatives gather to cheer the "warriors" to victory. State finals are especially well attended. The basketball teams from the Lodge Grass and Pryor high schools have won several state titles.

Banding together to fight political battles also gives the Crows a sense of unity. Many of these now take place in courtrooms. For instance, in the 1980s, the Crows filed a case against the government of Big Horn County, in which their reservation is located. Led by a young woman named Janine Pease Windy Boy, some tribe members claimed that the county had discriminated against several Crows. They demanded that the county's election system be changed so that tribe members would have a chance to become county officials. A federal judge agreed with them.

The Crows have won many other cases in non-Indian courts. These successes have inspired them to create their own court and elect their own judge. The tribal court now settles all disagreements among tribe members and keeps peace in the Crows' land.

The Crows hold their fair in August of each year. Its attractions include ceremonial dances, horse racing, rodeo riding, and the display of hundreds of tipis.

The Crows love to root for the champion basketball players from the high schools on their reservation.

Together, the Crow people have always worked hard to defend themselves and their homeland from enemies. The setting has changed from the battlefield to the courtroom, but their fighting spirit remains. That spirit has allowed the Crows to survive many hard times. And almost certainly it will help them thrive in the years to come. ▲

CHRONOLOGY

ca. 1000   Farm settlements are formed along the Missouri River in what is now North Dakota

ca. 1750   Two groups of Hidatsa Indians from the Missouri River valley move to the Yellowstone River valley to hunt; they become the Crow tribe

1806   Lewis and Clark explore the Crow homeland

1851   Crows and other Plains tribes meet with official of U.S. government at Fort Laramie and sign peace treaty

1868   Crows sign treaty granting the United States 30 million acres of their land

1880   Crow chiefs travel to Washington, D.C., and are compelled to sell United States 1.5 million more acres

1887   Respected Crow warrior Sword Bearer is killed by U.S. Army

1887-1904   U.S. government divides Crow Indian Reservation into individually owned plots called allotments

1911   Crows form business committee to represent tribe in official dealings with U.S. government

1934   U.S. government appoints tribal leader Robert Yellowtail as superintendent of the Crow reservation

1941   Religious leader William Big Day revives Sun Dance

1980s   Crows win court case against the government of Big Horn County

GLOSSARY

Absaroka   the Crows' name for themselves, meaning "Children of the Long-beaked Bird"

agent   an employee of the U.S. government responsible for conducting official business with an Indian tribe

allotment   U.S. policy of the late 1800s that sought to divide land owned by a tribe into small tracts owned by individuals; also, one of these tracts

band   a small group of Crows who lived and traveled together

clan   a group of Crow families, the members of which believed themselves to be very closely related

fur trade   trade network in which Indians gave non-Indians animal furs in exchange for metal tools and other machine-made goods

missionary   a person who tries to teach others about his or her religion

reservation   a tract of land set aside by the U.S. government for use by a specific group of Indians

tipi   a portable, cone-shaped dwelling made of a wooden frame covered by animal skins

tribe   a group of people that share a language, culture, and religious beliefs

INDEX

A

Absaroka, 16, 49. *See also* Crows
Agents, 52, 55, 57, 59, 60, 63
Agricultural fair, 63
Allotments, 61
Army, U.S., 50, 51–52, 59
Awatixa Hidatsa, 14, 15, 16. *See also*
Mountain Crows; River Crows; River

B

Bacheeitche, 21
Barcelo, Peter, 53
Basketball, 71
Bate, 25
Beckwourth, James, 41
Big Day, William, 70
Big Dogs (warrior society), 21
Bighorn Mountains, 62
Bighorn River, 32, 41, 49, 50, 53
Blackfoot, 44, 59
Black Lodge, 60
"Bloody Bozeman." *See* Bozeman Trail
Bows and arrows, 31
Bozeman Trail, 48, 49, 50, 51
Buffalo, 14, 18, 43, 47
Bureau of Indian Affairs (BIA), 53

C

Cheyennes, 43–44
"Children of the Long-beaked Bird,"
16. *See also* Crows
Christianity, 53, 63
Clans, 19–20, 21, 25
Clark, William, 32
Colter, John, 32
Congress, U.S., 60
Corn, 13–14
Creator, 22, 23, 25, 58
Crow Agency, 55, 59, 60, 71
Crow Fair, 71
Crow Indian Reservation, 50–51, 52,
53, 55, 57–63, 66, 67, 69
Crows
    and agriculture, 13, 52–53, 68

and allotment policy, 60–62
attitudes toward outsiders, 11
and buffalo, 14
ceremonies, 21–23, 57, 63, 70–
    71
creation myth, 7–11, 16
dwellings, 14, 18
early history, 14
education of children, 10, 23–24
family structure, 18
food, 13, 18
gender roles, 23–24
homeland, 11, 13, 32
and horses, 15, 21
language, 16
and non-Indians, 11, 27–29, 31–
    32, 41, 43, 50–51, 60
and Plains wars, 48–49, 51–52,
records of culture, 16
relations with other Plains
    tribes, 43–44, 48–49
tools, 31
tribal leadership, 19, 21
warrior societies, 20–21
weapons, 31–32

F

Fort C. F. Smith, 49
Fort Laramie, 44, 48, 50
Fort Laramie council (1851), 44–45,
    48
Fort Laramie treaty (1868), 51, 52
Fort Raymond, 41
Foxes (warrior society), 20
Fur traders, 27, 28, 43

G

General Allotment Act (1867), 60–61
Gold, 43, 47
Great Plains, 13, 14, 25, 29, 43, 44,
    47, 66
Guns, 29, 31

H

Hand game, 63

ABOUT THE AUTHOR

LEIGH HOPE WOOD is an editor and writer who lives in New York City. She holds a B.S. from Emory University and an M.A. in American studies from New York University. She has also written *The Navajo Indians* in Chelsea House's JUNIOR LIBRARY OF AMERICAN INDIANS.

PICTURE CREDITS